GHANA EMPIRE 7th – 12th Centuries

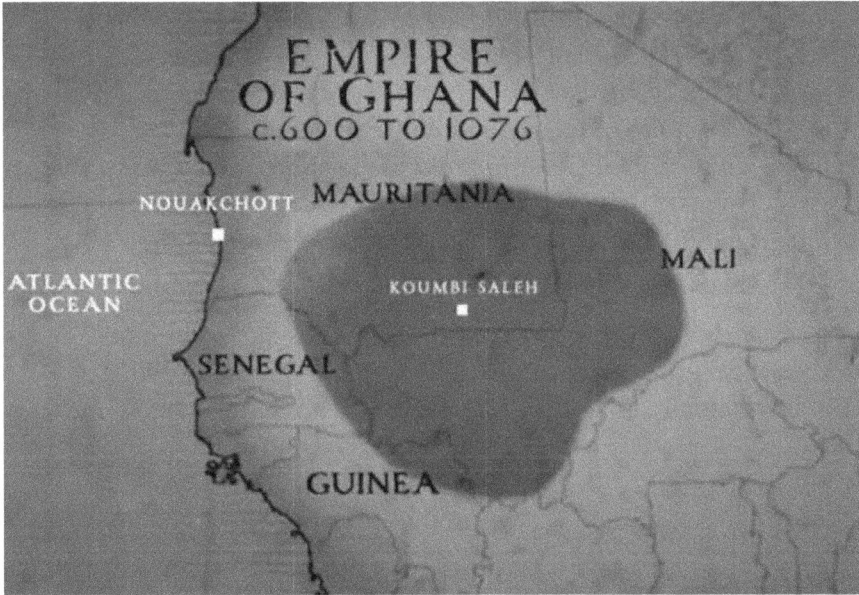

First West African Medieval Empire

Amadou Ba

From the Same Author

- *A Forgotten History: The Significant Contribution of Blacks Slaves and Soldiers to the Building of Canada 1604-1945*, AB Books, 2021.
- *Africa of Great Empires 7th-17th Centuries: A Thousand Years of Economic Prosperity, Political Unity, Social Cohesion and Cultural Influence*, AB Books, 2020.
- *Quelles Valeurs transmettre aux jeunes du 21e siècle? Ed. Essai pour Tous, Montréal, 2016.*

"Sénégalais" à Madagascar. Militaires ouest-africains dans la conquête et la colonisation de la Grande-Île (1895-1960), Ed. Harmattan, 2012.

Dedications

To my children and to all those who have supported and accompanied me in this project. I also dedicate this book to the conscious Pan-Africanist youth. To all those who want to know better what precolonial Africa was like, through its great medieval empires. To all the people of West Africa (Soninke, Mandingo, Fulani, Serer, Diola, Dogon, etc.) whose ancestors contributed to building this first medieval political state in the heart of Savannah and Sahel Africa. To all those who dream of one day seeing Africa become a federal state as powerful if not more than the great powers of the world today.

Acknowledgements

My very genuine thanks to all those who supported me in my research. You have devoted part of your precious time to the proofreading of my manuscript on the Africa of Great empires, from which this book is taken. Your corrections, suggestions, remarks, criticisms, and technical supports have been particularly useful to me. I particularly want to name: Sovi Lambert, Kristina Bernier and Dr Amélie Hien. I do not forget to associate my thanks with the following peoples: Junseo Lee for her decisive help in the design of the cover and the website and especially Anne Louise Heubi for her "coaching", her availability, and the quality design.

Quotes

"Until lions have their own historians, hunting stories will continue to glorify the hunter." (African proverb).

"Do not let go the fish you hold in your hand for the one you have under your feet" (Soninke proverb)

"If Africans do not talk about Africa, it will disappear". (Ousmane Sembene, a Senegalese writer, director, actor, and screenwriter)

"The negation of the history and intellectual achievements of black African peoples is the cultural, mental murder, which has already preceded and prepared the genocide here and there in the world". (Cheikh Anta Diop, historian, anthropologist, and Senegalese politician).

"If you abandon your spirituality to adopt that of your aggressor, you will become his slave forever." (Asian saying).

"Our only weakness is to ignore our strength." (Felwin Sarr, university professor, economist, philosopher, and pan-Africanist) extract from "Traces and speeches to African Nations", speech delivered on the opening of the Black Civilizations Museum on December 6, 2018, in Dakar, Senegal.

"The great medieval African empires teach us that what unites us is far stronger, more beautiful and truer than what disunites us". (Amadou Ba, historian, researcher, and writer).

"When we spoke of friendship, declared the hyena: "Friendship for a day, it is not difficult, even I can practice it". But friendship is not an affair of one day. Formerly Friendship survived with friends, but nowadays it is friendship that dies leaving friends to live.

GHANA EMPIRE 7th — 12th Centuries   Amadou Ba

PLAN

INTRODUCTION

The Questions of Sources

Arab Sources

West African Oral Sources on the Origin of Ghana

Archaeological Sources on the Origin of Ghana Empire

The Beginning of the Ghana Empire

The Soninke: The African People Who Have Paved the Way

Ghana a very Prosperous Empire

Ghana Country of Gold

Ghana, the Backbone of the Trans-Saharan Trade

Ghana: A Military Force

Political and Social Organization of Ghana Empire

A Common Currency in the Vast Empire of Ghana: Cowries

Ghana's Decline

Conclusion

Bibliography

INTRODUCTION

It is thanks to the modern archaeological excavations[1], to the Arabic travelers during the medieval epoch and above all the African ancestral oral tradition which has been handed generations to generations for centuries[2] that has made it possible to know the first of the African great empires of the Middle Age period: Wagadu[3] (or Ouagadou) as it was called by its people, but its famous name is Ghana[4] throughout the Muslim world and Europe. (Diagana, 2011).

The Ghana Empire is an African state which has its golden age days between the 7th and the 11th centuries in West Africa. Though, its origins go back to a more remote period. It was situated between the upper waters of the Senegalese river valley and the one of Niger, more precisely in the zone situated

---

[1] The Sahelian archaeological excavations have shown that the Mandingo who living there were organized in small colonies around 1000 before our Era. Around 600 before our Era, it existed vast villages and from 400 to 900 after Christ we noticed many urban centers in the Sahel region. One of them was called Koumbi Saleh, which was the capital city of the empire of the founded by the Soninke people, according to the archaeologists.

[2] See about the topic: the decisive book of Germaine Dieterlen and Diarra Sylla, *The Empire of Ghana: The Wagadu and the Yerere tradition* published in the edition Khartala, Paris, 1992.

[3] The term Wagadu means « cattle city » or according to another hypothesis « the Wague's Land » the suffix « du » is a term which belongs to the Mandingo language from which the Soninke is part of it means « city », it is found in many west African places (such as Burkina Faso, Ouagadougou, or Kedougou in the West of Senegal too.) The term Waga may refer to « cattle » or referring to the Wague Clan / reigning families.

[4] This term comes from the Soninke people (nwana which is pronounced nana or Ghana in The Soninke). It signifies «hero »/big warrior).

between the East of Senegal, the South of Mauritania and the West of Mali.

Koumbi Saleh, one of its most prosperous cities, was also its capital. We must not confuse the Ghana Empire with the current West African country which has the same name; it is a former British colony, the Gold Coast. It was named Ghana in 1957, when Gold Coast got its independence, the reason of naming the country Ghana, was to pay tribute to the well-known first African empire.

The nomination by the President Kwame Nkrumah[5] intended also to show a total rupture with the British colony and to invite his African counterparts to find a strong federal country which was the only and unique way to reach development, economic, political, and even military independence.

Ghana, which we are discussing in this book is not to be confused with the Nkrumah's country, and to be more precise, it is not even in the same geographical region. Besides, the Ghana Empire was larger than the present Ghana and has lasted more than 700 years during the medieval period. Because of the fact, the African Black Empire is not well-known, it seems essential to ponder over it, through these several pages, because this first sub-regional state constituted a pride for the Sub-Saharan people. Its founders, expansion, flourishing time in a vast space of the Savannah and the African Sahara, its agricultural and mineral richness, the flourishing trade, the political organization, its cultural influences, the relations with

---

[5] Born on September 21st, 1909, in Nhroful (former Gold Coast British colony), Kwame N'Krumah died on April 27, 1972. He was a great separatist and man of State, a pan Africanist. N'Krumah was the leader of the movement for the independent of Ghana. When this British colony became independent, N'krumah became the first as prime minister from 1957 to 1960 and the as the President (1960-1966).

the exterior world, specifically with the Arabic world[6], and finally its decline are points that will be clarified in this study.

---

[6] This so-called Arabo- Muslim civilization has concerned since the birth of this new religion (Islam) in the 7th century of our Era till the 15th Century many countries from the Far East to the Near West; from China to Andalusia, until the expulsion of Muslims and as well as the Jewish from the year 1492 and many others. They were countries who had political, esthetical, religious, and juridical framework of life the Arabic language and not as an ethnic group. Islam was dominant religion there, and the domination was without any exclusion based on languages, cultures, and religions, etc. For example, the Jewish, Christian, Egyptian, Greek, Latin, etc. to whom the Arabo-Muslim owe much their science, literature, philosophy, medicine, mathematics, astronomies, translation, and works' transmission.

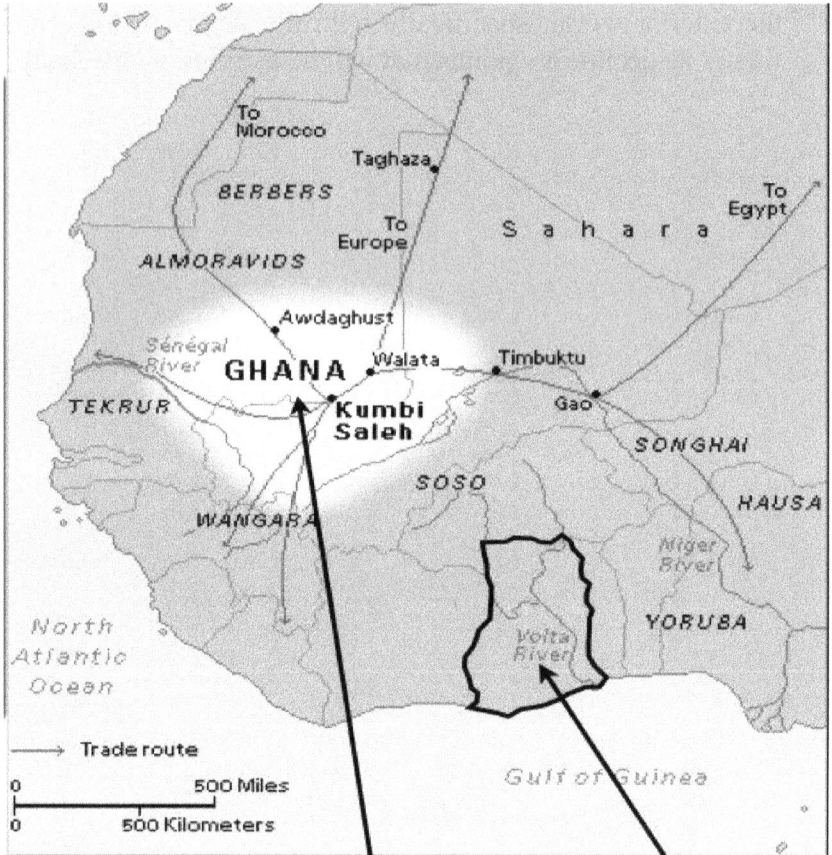

Ghana Empire, 830-1235

Modern Ghana

https://janakesho1.wordpress.com/2016/01/23/old-ghana-empire-wagadou/

The Questions of Sources

For this study three types of sources have contributed to better understand the African medieval empire, Ghana. We have first the sources produced by Arabic geographers and followed by the oral African tradition and the recent contribution of archeological sources.

Arab Sources

An array of geographers and other Arabic authors have produced manuscripts on the African continent, noticeably in the East part and the Savannah, the Sahel between the middle of 9th and 11th centuries. We can quote some among them:

Ibn Khordadhbeh, Yakub (m. 897), al Masudi (m. 965), Ibn Hawkal (m. 977), al-Burini (UNESCO Magazine, June 1974). Yakub, who has travelled throughout Egypt and Maghreb, and he has summarized the essential of his travel. This painting is both in his *Tarikh* and *Buldan* (edited by Bibliotheca Geographumarabicorum, t, VII of Goeje) like most Arabic geographers. The Translation of G. Wist, published under the title the *Countries' Book,* is useful but not always precise, it informs us a lot on the Black continent: in Ethiopia, Sudan, Nubia, the Bejja, and the Zendy. In Sudan, he mentions the Zghawa of Kamen and depicts their habitations and describes the important kingdom of Ghana.

The *Masalik* (*Kitab al-Masalikwa-l-Mamalik*, B.G. A. II; the Kubel and the V. Matveiev, II 33 and following) of Ibn Hawkal are more detailed. He has visited the Nubia and perhaps the West Sudan. His depiction is much more interesting because of the idea that he has made concerning the commercial relations between Maghreb and Sudan. We can note that all the other geographers are informed on North Africa.

Ibn al Fakih about Ghana and Kuki, the traveler Buzurg Ibn Shariyar about the East Coast and the Zendi, Muhallabi as for him, he has saved in his treaty some fragments of Uswarii. And finally, the golden prairies of Masudi (m. 965) are filled with information about the Zendi and the East coast. These texts have earlier interested the students of African races and even eastern specialist such as Delafosse, Currili (*Documentiarabi per la storia dell Ethiopia*, 1931), Kramers (*Djughrafiya Islamic Encyclopedia, the Eritrea which was described in an Arabic source dated in the tenth century, Atti del XIX Congressodegliorentalisti, Rome*, 1938). Among the above sources, we have documents, manuscripts, or books gathering the following categories: columns, news reports, geographies and journeys, legal and religious books, literary texts, etc. Al Bakri 's *Masalik and Namalik* embody the geographical understanding's peak about Maghreb and Ghana. Even if, Al Bakri has not travelled in these regions, he has fittingly used Al- Warraq's notes, yet these ones are not today available both for those the traders and the travelers. We can clearly note that, the contribution of Arabic authors in the understanding of Ghana, North Africa, the Sahel, and the Savannah, is of a paramount importance, even though sometimes their writings might have some shortcomings.

But, when we compare them with other sources such as the African oral tradition, this can help us to better understand it.

West African Oral Sources on the Origin of Ghana

The first attempt for a rational organization of research concerning oral tradition in Africa were undertaken within the framework of the project to write the General History of Africa which was adopted during the UNESCO's Fourteenth General

Lecture's session. Lectures which have been held in Abidjan (Ivory Coast), in Niamey (Niger) and Ouagadougou (Burkina Faso) during the following years have made people think about the necessity to create regional research centers for oral tradition.

The summary of works based on these diverse discussions was recorded in a book edited by D. Laya (1972). (Gomgnimbou, and Juhe-Beaulation, 2006). These decisions despite having come late, have contributed to better understand the African history noticeably the one of the great medieval empires. As for Ghana, there are oral sources whose holders are the wise people or the storytellers whose role is to transmit the oral traditions in the West African societies. Those we are talking about here are totally different from todays, who are just playing the role of praising ministers, presidents, or famous personalities.

The great majority of nowadays storytellers in West Africa have neither any role in the transmission of history nor in the building of collective memory and a sincere oral patrimony. However, they act as swindlers, only interested by money. In this book, it is about the storytellers who are holders of oral traditions' holders coming from all different ethnic groups in the west African Region: the Mandingo, the Fulani, the Soninke etc. They have talked about the Ghana empire, and the epoch during which their ancestors were living there. These oral sources have for a long time been neglected in the favor of written sources. The oral sources on Ghana after having been scattered everywhere, have finally been gathered by several authors among whom Germaine Dieterlen and Diarra Sylla in their book: *The Ghana Empire, the Wagadu and the Yerere traditions* or even the one of Youba Bathily in his book entitled: The Ghana Empire's roots of Ghana Empire.

Archaeological Sources on the Origin of Ghana Empire

The archeological sources have also contributed to better understand the Ghana Empire. Archaeological excavations have started being carried out since the early years of the 20th century; these excavations occurred noticeably in the site of its Capital Koumbi (Kumbi) Saleh. The archaeological sources exploited in 1913, showed that Koumbi Saleh was the capital of Ghana Empire in the sixth century. It was in the south part of the present Mauritania, the Soninke country. This shows a clear proof that, it was the Soninke who have founded the Kingdom of Wagadu which became later the great empire between the 7th and 12th centuries.

Besides, we also have information about trade between Ghana and Maghreb thanks to the archaeological investigations. Beyond that, these sources inform that Kumbi Saleh was the salt and gold deposit in relation with the North Africa. Kumbi Saleh had nearly 3000 inhabitants in the 11th Century. Its political organization is not mentioned. In a word, the combination of the three sources: manuscripts of Arabic authors, West African oral tradition and archaeological sources have helped to rebuild the former Ghana Empire's history.

The Beginning of the Ghana Empire

There are several versions about the Wagadu's origins. According to the West African oral traditions, the "Wagadu" the heart of the empire might have been founded around the third century before J.C, by an armed conflict coming from the East and led by Dinga Cissé (Sisay). Yet, for the others, the origin of Ghana goes back around 500 after J.C. The written texts on the origin of Ghana were handed to us by Arabic geographers who were living in the North and Spain[7]. These documents are the most widespread and older ones and have survived until nowadays.

In these manuscripts written by Arabic-speaking columnist, their authors defend that the Kingdom might have been founded by the farming Black people, the Soninke[8], they were animist, and live in the Saharan South border. According to the *Tarikh-es-Sudan* "the History of Sudan", the foundation of Ghana might have been in the third century by Black people who were farmers. The Arabic authors knew already the existence of Ghana in the 8th century in the South of Sahara thanks to these sources. They have also heard that it was a great river in Sudan; therefore, the word "Sudan" is derived from *Bilad Al Sudan*.

The Muslim- Arabic have named the zone which covers the Sub-Saharan West African Savannah "*Bilad- al- sudan*" which means "The Country of Black people" in the Arabic language. The West African Savannah has become the West Sudan because of the earlier use of the Arabic term. This foresaid Sudan is opposed to East Sudan which gather nowadays two (Sudan and the South Sudan). These two countries formed one until July 2011 the date when South Sudan became independent, yet the other regions of this part of Africa which were inhabited by dark-skinned people. The first reference

---

[7]Al-Andulus (Andalusia) was the term that was used to name all the territories of the Iberian Peninsula and some of the South of France which were once under Islamic domination between 711 and 1942 (in all 781 years). Andalusia which is derived from its name was only for a longtime small part of it.

[8] It is an Arabic manuscript whose author is Abderrahmane Es Saadi around 1650. The book is about the great West African Empires. It constitutes one of the two history references book about West Africa with *Tarikh el-Fettach*.

related to the origin of Ghana is to be attributed to the Arabic astronomer Muhammad al-Fazari[9] during the 7th century.

He was cited by Al-Mas'udi in his book *Murujjadh-dhahab* (The golden prairies). He evokes in the book, (Ghana; the land of Gold[10]). Another Arabic geographer, Al-Bakri[11], in his geographical description of the known world, written much more later, in the 11th century, relates the Ghana history too.

The region where which the empire of Ghana spread out is characterized by vast grasslands, giant trees, which are widely spread, the seasonal precipitations, and the river Niger, with its numerous tributaries. The Arabic geographers considered it might be the Nile that they knew in the Northeast of Africa, the part where which it crossed the River Egypt. They understood that the Nile was exceedingly long, and it was originated so far from the entrails of Africa, though they have never been there. Nowadays, the Nile has its source in the deep heart of Africa, precisely from the Victoria Lake (Uganda, Kenya, and Tanzania). This one is the White Nile. The other rises in the Lake Tana (Ethiopia); it is the Blue Nile. The Arabic authors, who have never been in the tropical regions of the continent, knew only this part of Nile. They did not know the other waterways inside the continent. They have never heard about

---

[9] Abou Abdallah Muhammad ibn Ibrahim al Fazal (died in 796 or 806) is a Muslim astronaut. He is author of the book Indian Astronomia which was translated into Arabic. Mas'udi as for him he was born in Bagdad in Iraq at the end of the 9th century and died in Fostat (956). He was an Arabic encycopdepist and photograph at this time of the Islam's peak. His Muruj-adh-dhahabwa-ma'din al-jawhar, (Golden Prairies and Mines of Precious Stones) remained until the middle of the 15th century the reference book for Arabic and Persian geographers and historians.

[10] « The Cambridge History of Africa Volume 2: From c.500 BC to AD 1050, p. 651 », published in May 2013.

[11] Abu UbaydAbd Allah ibnAbd al-Aziz ibn Muḥammad al-Bakriou or Abu Ubayd al-Bakri, geographer, and historian of the Muslim Hispania (Al-Andalus), he was born in 1014 in Huelva. Son of the Taïfa Emire from Huelva and Saltes, al-Bakrihas spent a major part of his life in Cordoba where he died in 1094.

the Niger River, his name Joliba (its mandingo, mande, malinke name), a large waterway, more than 4000 km, one of the largest in Africa.

The Wagadu Kingdom of the Soninke has gradually become an empire under the influence of Cissé (Siseh) Tounkara's dynasty whose catalysis is Kaya Maghan Cissé (Siseh). The famous Ghanaian kings are: Dinga Cissé (Siseh) who reigned around 750. The others that we do not know have reigned between 800 and 1040, we have also Riyo (1040-1062), Menin (1062-1076), the Diarisso's dynasty with more than sovereigns (1087 and 1180).

After this occupation, comes the Kanté (Kanteh), Soumaoro. The rapid expansion of Wagadu is due to its golden richness (Kaya Maghan, the emperor title which means at the same time golden Master) but also to its political organization, iron work by its blacksmiths and more importantly because of the fact, it has conquered all the small neighboring kingdoms, which it added one by one for the building of a great empire around the 8th Century (Diagana, 2011). From that epoch to approximately to the end of the 12th Century, Ghana was the most powerful empire in the Savannah Region and the West Sahelian Africa.

Its recognition as an empire is attributed to the Arabic historian and geographer Ahmad al Yaqubi [12] and among others. The latter has depicted the Ghanaian sovereign like an emperor, an enormously powerful leader on whom subordinated kings

---

[12] Ahmad ibn Abu Ya'qubibnJa' far ibn Wadih al- Ya'qubi (?-897) known with the name al-yaqubi), is an Arabic historian and geographer, author of the World history: ta'rikhibnwadih (Chronique Ibn Wadih) and the general geography, Kitab –al-buldan(countries book) it particularly describes Bagdad and Samarra. He was Wadih's grandson freed by Califal Mansur. He lives in Armenia and Khorasan until 873 under the patronage of Tarirides Iranian Dynasty, history of which, he has written. After the fall of Tahirides, he travelled from India to Maghreb and then died in Egypt undoubtedly in West Africa. He evokes Ghana as an Empire.

depended, and reined in a vast territory consisting of different provinces which are gathered in a space formed by several West African states.

The Soninke: The African People Who Have Paved the Way

Today, if the Soninke do not occupy a remarkable place in the West African countries because of the lack of representation in any of post-colonial or their language is neglected compared to other languages such as Wolof in Senegal, Bambara in Mali, Sose in Gambia, or Hassanya in Mauritania, etc.; yet this has never been the case talking about these Soninke, who have built the Ghana empire. They were also traders, farmers, blacksmiths, and migrant who, today, live in many West African countries and in the Diaspora. Talking about ethnicity or linguistics, they represent the North group of the Mandingo[13]. They are often mixed with other groups, and they are mostly found in the high valley. In Mali, they represent 10% of the population, yet in Senegal they are just 2%. They live in the South of Mauritania and Burkina Faso too.

Today, they can be estimated around more than 1.5 million in West Africa. The Soninke ethnic group is divided into sub-groups: the group that we can consider authentic ones which main activity is agriculture is added the Markas or Marakas and certain other group: the Dioula whose main activity is trade[14].

---

[13]Mandingues and Malinkes peoples: two Mande's West African sub-groups they founded the greatest west African Empires. Among them we have the Soninkes, the Soussous, the Bambara, the Dioulas and the Samos. The smallest groups constitute the Ligbis, the Vais and the Bisas.

[14] As far as this topic/subject: one must refer to the study entitled: some anthropologists 'books on the Soninke published in the French Sociology Review 1978-19-2- pp. 295-298, or the Germaine Dieterlen and Mamadou Soumare Book: The empire of Ghana : The Wagadu and the Yerere Traditions (Published in french under the title *L'empire du Ghana: le Wagadu et les traditions Yerere*).

The commercial ambition of the Wangara or Dioula dates before the arrival of the Arabs (Niane,1980,142).

The one of the greatest fames of the Soninke is still being these great traders which goes back to the epoch of the Ghana Empire. At the beginning of the first century of the Middle age, they had not only been in contact with different ethnic groups of the West African Savannah but also with the Saharan nomads from whom they acquired some horses brought from North Africa. Their iron arms and dominant horses have helped the first Soninke to establish an empire. They have progressively spread their territories and dominated the neighboring leaders, which has permitted the kingdom to become an empire as it is earlier mentioned.

Ghana a very Prosperous Empire

The Ghana Empire was economically extraordinarily rich. This has been mentioned in the written sources. The oral tradition has clarified it too. The prosperity of Ghana has been possible thanks to a dynamic and diverse economy which was held at the same time by prosperous agriculture, mineral and an abundance of natural resources, with exchange which are not only internal with different provinces but also external with the Maghreb and the Arabic world etc.

First, in the agricultural field, it is important to note that a great majority of the Ghana empire takes advantage of a strategic geographical position which favors a productive and abundant agriculture. Indeed, in the South, West-east parts of this vast and federal State, fertile lands, and many waterways were available, and they permit to harvest many times in the year.

The rivers rising, added to wintry rains created an adequate situation for the diversity of the crops. These advantages have made possible for excellent harvesting and even some excess.

Therefore, the Ghanaian farmers have the possibility to exchange their surplus with the neighboring populations. The exchange was not only in the interior of the empire but with the exterior precisely with Berber tribes, the Moorish, the Tuareg, and with the Muslims world until the Arabia.

The availability of fertile lands irrigated or being watered by rain have therefore enabled the first occupants of this vast region of west Sudan to devote themselves to agriculture to exploit their natural resources and to build a brilliant civilization. Thus, the Ghanaians populations have passed through the prehistoric survival of hunting and gathering to a more reliable production for living. We can consider the Nile as being «Egypt is a gift» as we consider the Ghana being a natural gift of the West African Savannah and above all for the two big rivers of the region, the current Niger River, Senegal River. In fact, the annual floods of these following rivers: Joliba, (Niger), Senegal (and its tributary, the Faleme), Gambia etc., deposit a rich yellow layer which turns the region into an extremely fertile productive, agricultural zone. Besides, during the last centuries with the advance of cultivating lands, state rivalries, many peasants have therefore quarreled the historic belonging of this space in this rich environment. Their objective was to practice food crops to face the unfair competition of culture crops which were introduced by colonizers.

Even recently, the West African nations quarrel between themselves for the control of certain rich and irrigated lands by rivers which are filled with histories, storytelling, myths, and legends. As for example it is the conflict which have opposed the Mauritanians Moorish against the Black people of the country, but also between Senegal and Mauritania or the question in relation to the borders and to the access of cultivated lands and between Mauritania and Mali for the same reasons.

Apart from the prosperous harvest of the Ghanaian populations, there were also very fertile meadows in the savannah which facilitate breeding. The breeders were lucky to have green spaces where their cattle could stray. After agriculture, the dominant element is the breeding. It has contributed to making Ghana an empire economically prosperous. Indeed, there is a various use for all the shepherds or agro-pastors, in the East as in the West of African continent. It is clearly stated that cattle constitute wealth as Melville Herskovits, underlined it in his long article –Cattle complex in the East Africa[15] (Herskovits 1926, p 650). Beyond that, he shows how important the cattle are in his study area. The geographical cattle complex that he considers is essential.

Though, his article discusses the breeding in the East societies of the African continent. It is obvious to admit the analysis confirms the breeding in West Africa precisely during the Ghana empire epoch, but also in the empire which came after it. Some inhabitants of the former Ghanaian empire namely the Fulani are great cattle breeders. The former with other people practiced a fruitful cattle breeding of sheep, goats, and above all cows for centuries or millenaries.

Products from the breeding completes the agricultural yields of the sedentary farmers which consisted of cereals such as millet, fonio, sorghum, but also fruits vegetables like sweet potato melon etc. The surplus of production is for the exchanges with

---

[15] « Aire de la vache » is the French correct translation of the phrase « cattle complex », who after the article of Herskovits has succeeded thanks to the pastoral societies' literature.

23

the neighboring people using the bartering system (dairy products with millet for instance).

Beyond the agriculture, the breeding, the fishing, craft-industry, and the trade[16], were developed sectors in the Ghana empire that all Arabic geographers have mentioned and concluded that the existence of great urban centers precisely in the outskirts of the large rivers was due to this economic prosperity.

Regarding this precise description, Ghana can be among these empires, because the great majority of the great world civilizations have been built on the vast waterways' banks[17]. We also note the existence of populous villages and even towns in the former Ghana Empire.

The Arabic authors talk about it in their writings, but they are the only ones to account for it at a time when a good part of humanity was in a rudimentary economy, in wars and famines including territories of the greatest powers of the contemporary world.

Indeed, archeological investigations have shown that in middle of the second century of our era, an urban population has developed in certain places of what would be fully part of the Ghana empire. In the region of Jene in the current Mali for instance Jenne-Jeno in the flood plain between Niger and Bani urban centers, which go to the epoch of Ghana, have been found there. Jenne-Jeno thanks to its geographical situation, has

---

[16] We will be back on the importance of trade in Ghana when it comes to talk the exchanges with the Arab-Muslims. We will then analyze the importance of craftsmanship through the mastery of iron when we will be talking about the military question of the Ghanaian Empire.

[17] The Egyptian civilization on the Nile bank, the Arab- Persian civilization on the Tigre and Euphrates bank, the European civilization on the Seine, Po, or the Thames bank and even on the Saint Lawrence, the Canadian great cities (Quebec, Rimouski, Montreal, Three Rivers, etc. In the case if we want to make a link with which has passes here in our welcoming country.

become one of the first West Sudan cities, this took place probably at the time when Koumbi Saleh became the center for the Soninke people in the West of Ghana Empire.

Apart from the richness generated by the farming abundance and the products derived from the breeding, Ghana's economy success is mainly due to its resources derived from its subsoil such as iron, particularly gold. The Empire was rich to the point that, it was nicknamed by Arab Geographers and oriental travelers as the country of Gold.

Ghana Country of Gold

Gold is linked to the birth of and importance of Ghana. The latter was described as one of the most fortunate places in terms of gold in the world during the Middle Age. The gold and iron mines are inexhaustible. "The country of Gold" corresponds to the gold-bearing region of the Bambuk and Bure which stretches the authority of the Ghana's sovereign. Gold and iron are still being exploited in abundantly even today in West African countries in which Bambuk and Bure are part of. It is particularly the East of Senegal, the West of Mali, the South of Mauritania or in Guinea and Burkina Faso which are now being exploited by the greatest mining companies in the world particularly Canadians, Americans, French, Australians, Chinese, and even Indians.

In fact, what has caught the attention of Arab geographers with a strong desire to visit Ghana or to leave written testimonies, were the stories they heard from travelers and traders. The people the Arab writers have interviewed or from whom they heard the story had all mentioned fabulous riches in Ghana particularly the huge quantities of gold. Thus, at the end of the 8th century AD, the Arab astronomer and scholar Ibrahim al-Fazari called Ghana "the country of gold". N. Levtzion and JFP

25

Hopkins in their Corpus of Early Arabic Sources for West African History, repeated what al-Fazari has mentioned about Ghana but also what others believed like Al-Hasan ibn Ahmad al-Hamdani (around 893 - 945), who stated that the richest gold mine in the world was in Ghana. For Arab geographers like al-Hamdani, Ghana was a mysterious place of darkness beyond the sources of the "Nile" where there were "waters that grow gold" (Levtzion and Hopkins). All the Arab writers were unanimous, affirming and repeating in their accounts that Ghana was a land of wealth, and that gold was in abundance there.

Some Arab writers even had exaggerated ideas about the gold, which was in abundance, waiting to be picked up and brought home. For example, the classical writer ibn al-Faqih al Hamadhani (d. 912) said: "In Ghana, gold grows in the sand like carrots, and it is picked at sunrise." Towards the end of the 10th century, the anonymous author of *Akhbar al-Zaman* stated approximately at the end of the 10th Century, that traders would sneak into the kingdom of Ghana where "all the earth is gold". He added: "The people of Ghana would light fires, melt the precious metal and fly away with it." The same author has reported a traveler in Ghana who found "places where golden rods grew" (cited in Levtzion and Hopkins). We also know that such tales have lasted for a long time, because in the 14th century when Ghana experienced its decline and was integrated into the Mali Empire and then into the Songhai Empire, the Syrian historian and geographer al-Umari (1301-1349) further described two types of plants that had golden roots. It is for this reason that the Muslim world and the Arab conquerors were going to take a great interest in this region of Africa to later take possession of the immense wealth. This practise is not a new one, even today when we see the world's most powerful countries rush towards Africa to take control of the mining, energy, and agricultural potentials, to the point of supporting dictators and potentates who far from being presidents democratically elected by the populations, are only servants and sub-prefects of the strongest in this world on the continent.

The ideas of geographers about the abundance of gold in the former Ghana Empire, is reinforced by oral tradition among all West African ethnicities who were part of this vast empire. Even today, the populations of the Senegal River valley call the pure gold under the Galam, which is the region located in the Eastern part of Senegal on the border with Mali. It is in this very region that large foreign companies (American, Canadian, Australian and Chinese) are competing for operating contracts with the State of Senegal to achieve huge profits through the transformation of this yellow metal, particularly in jewellery, electronics, financial products, aerospace or even the medical sector, the manufacture of glass and building facades, etc., without respecting ecological standards nor rewarding fairly the poor populations (including women and children) who work there in miserable and inhumane conditions.

Endowed with enormous agricultural, mining, livestock, and artisanal products thanks to the mastery of iron and gold work by its blacksmiths, Ghana was seeing its ambitions increasing. Therefore, it has developed a vast network of commercial exchanges with particularly the Berbers of the Sahara and all the Arab populations thereafter. Trade, especially trans-Saharan through trade with Arab-Muslim populations, was resplendent. On a vast territory which stretched from middle Senegal to the West, around what would later become Timbuktu in the East, Ghana had something to offer and exchange with its trading partners.

Ghana, the Backbone of the Trans-Saharan Trade

Among the various factors which have ultimately transformed the kingdom of Soninke of Wagadu to an empire, there is also and above all its control of regional and trans-Saharan trade. The state of Ghana, according to the oldest testimonies of geographers, was based on the control of trade routes, especially those of gold. It was indeed, for the Arabs, the country per excellence of this Sudanese gold whose role would be essential in the economy of Mediterranean Islam and medieval[18] Europe. However, the trans-Saharan trade, centered on this precious metal, remained insignificant during Antiquity and has only been organized by Muslim caravanners in the 8th century. It was then that the commercial metropolis of Sijilmasa appeared in southern Morocco, a counterpart to Awdaghost, one of the Berber towns conquered and occupied by Ghana for several centuries. The Regional trade involved the exchange of several products that played a major role in the daily life of populations. This is the case of salt for instance.

The history of this food begins to take on a real importance from the moment when man tries to get involved in the effective production of this food and its conservation in all seasons. Today with our sophisticated freezers and refrigerators, we have not realized that things have not always been so for the peoples and civilizations that came before us. In addition to preserving food, salt is especially important for the human species as for all living species. In humans, for example, salt deficiency can lead to coma and even death[19]. Salt is also a good

---

[18] The Trans-Saharan networks of the Golden and slave trade during the 8th century of the Middle Age in the Magazine: *L'année du Maghreb*, VII, 2011, File: Sahara en Mouvement. Research document : Sahara en Mouvement: Le Sahara dans l'histoire.
[19] Available on these websites:
https://journals.openedition.org/anneemaghreb/1106#tocto1n1

spice makes a menu consisting mainly of vegetables. In the past, it has facilitated the adoption of agriculture and animal breeding and its use has spread to other techniques which are specific to a sedentary way of life (making leather, polishing pottery). It is therefore one of the pillars of the Neolithic revolutions and hence of civilizations. If this element is one of the most targeted products in the trade between Ghana and its partners, we can say that it is not by chance. Being in the mines of the Sahara Desert very often in territories controlled by the Berbers, the emperor of Ghana did not hesitate to run after this precious matter through his conquest or the trade of exchange. Beyond, salt, Ghana received from its Saharan trade partners copper and dates. But the most luxurious and desired was the horse.

Indeed, in these trans-Saharan exchanges, the Moslem conquerors brought horses which they exchanged with products that Ghana had. Because of its geographical position (see map above map), Ghana was well placed to dominate the international trade of caravans through Western Sahara and the Middle East but through the Mediterranean Sea too. One of the most important reasons of this commercial development has been the introduction of the camel into North Africa. This animal has played a paramount role in the existence of the trans-Saharan trade. Called the desert ship; due to its unique physiological characteristics, it can survive in very arid climates. With its large, flat feet well suited for manoeuvring through sands, the camel could carry large loads for several days without food or water.

If Ghana received products that it had not through trade with the populations of North Africa in return allowed its Arab-

---

https://www.passeportsante.net/fr/Actualites/Dossiers/DossierComplexe.aspx?doc=sel-poison-le-sel-un-nutriment-trop-utile

Muslim trading partners to acquire products from the West African savannah that they did not have. These products include, for example, cattle, iron tools, handcrafted weapons, utensils, animal hides, leather goods such as sandals, cushions, and bags, woven and dyed fabrics. Locally clayed pottery, woven grass products such as baskets and sleeping mats, herbal medicines, cola nuts and foodstuffs such as dried fish, rice, various cereals, condiments, spices, honey, and fruit. In the South, next to the forest, there were gold and cola nuts too.

Although gold was the product per excellence, the one that made Ghana famous in the medieval Arab world and in Europe, it must be noted that the cola nut also occupied a major place in the commercial circuits of the Ghana Empire. The cola nut or cola (or kola) is the seed of trees of the genus Cola, generically named colatier (or kolatier), represented mainly by Cola *nitida* and Cola *acuminata*. Coming from the tropical forest of West and Central Africa, it has long been appreciated by local populations for its stimulating properties, due to its high caffeine content. It is freshly eaten while being stripped of its pulpy integuments; it is chewed for a long time in the mouth where it first develops an astringent and bitter flavor and then the sweet. Symbol of benevolence, it also holds an important place in the habits and customs of the society. Even today, no marriage or birthday celebration is celebrated in West Africa without the distribution of cola nuts.

Produced in the tropical forests which stretch from current Guinea-Bissau to current Ghana, it has been exported to the North for centuries, by caravans of Dioulas[20] or Wangaras[21] carriers, to the region of the western Sudanese savannah.

---

[20] According to the ethnologist Amadou H.B, the (Jula) Dioulas were wandering traders who were present in the whole West African, this time corresponds to the influencing period of the Mandingo. There are the Bambaras, the Mandingo.
[21]

(Delafosse, 1912). The trade was practised with a far-away distance, and then spread eastward in the contemporary Nigeria. Nowadays and especially in Western countries, the cola nut has been made famous by the carbonated drink by an American Atlanta pharmacist. Cola or rather cola nut. Having understood, that cola nut is a powerful stimulant primarily intended to fight against physical and intellectual tiredness, an American company has taken lots of advantage from it with the carbonated drink Coca-Cola. Who does not know Coca-Cola today? But who knows the origin of the true history of cola? Another proof that today what positive and good Africa brings to the world is very often ignored or overlooked.

As far as the Muslim's expansion spread in the Maghreb, and in the West African afterwards, another element is introduced in the trade affairs: slavery. (Trans-Saharan slave trade).

Slavery became a current practice which was imposed by the new chiefs. Finally, it progressively became a current practice in the Ghanaian and later Malian, Songhay populations' habits, behaviours, as it will be stated in the following pages. Indeed, the numerous contests, the desire to acquire richness, the new armies (or unknown armies), luxurious products and above the horses where were brought from the farthest Mongolia through the exchanges that they were practising with East people, made the Ghanaians populations to integrate slavery in the trans-Saharan trade. This will constitute one of the destructive elements of the social cohesion in the Ghana Empire and even its disintegration too. Before coming to it later, let us note Ghana succeeded in becoming a military power with a well-organized and a numerous army during its most beautiful period of its peak.

Ghana: A Military Force

What is lacking in Africa today, Wagadu had succeeded 1,200 years ago, which is establishing a federal state based on a united and solid army, with equipment supply from or was made by the blacksmiths who transformed iron which was extracted in the different territories. Indeed, the mastery of iron for tools and weapons as well as the subsequent acquisition of horses through exchanges with the Arab Muslims allowed certain people of Sudan and during the time of the Ghana Empire to deploy superior armies and dominate others. This is more significant since we were at a time when Europe was unable to do so and was going through difficult economic periods accentuated by endless rivalries and wars. Here are facts, a difficult reality for the *twenty-first century homo to admit.*

With this disciplined and available army, the most powerful king of Wagadu formed an empire by conquering his weaker rivals and adding their land and commercial income to his domain. The regiments of Ghana included cavalry, tanks, and foot infantry. The warriors were all armed with throwing weapons, spears, or poisonous bows and arrows. They often built their tanks themselves too. These were noticeably light: the rims were made with an assembly of three branches of *nombo* wood, a kind of flexible and strong rattan, surrounded by leather straps. The spokes were four, the hubs, the axle, the drawbar were made of kapok wood as well as a small platform covered with leather. It supported a single warrior with a bow (grave), a quiver containing arrows (*gundayi*). The chariot was pulled by a single horse[22]. When the fighters of the Emperor of

---

[22]The Wangaras' origin goes back to the Kingdom of Wagadu. They were called the Wakore and had the privilege from the king to practice the trade of gold powder. According to the Guinean historian Djibril Tamsir NIANE, the word Wangara "Ouangara" designs for the Fulani, the Hawsas (Haoussa) the Mandens (Mandingue). Wangara and Wakores have the same origin whatever the fact that the

Ghana wanted to take a village, the war drum was first beaten, because they did not attack without warning the enemy. These horseback scouts who are armed with spears set out first. The galloping chariots followed them and circled the town, turning in the reverse of a clock needle so that the fitter could stretch his bow with his right hand. They are followed by or helped by footed archers, who captured all the enemies once defeated by them, and set fire on the populations using their flaming arrows. So, when the combatants were defeated, the regions they had occupied, organized the empire, they renounced warlike enterprises and integrated the populations into their political entity. However, they still have a simple army and horsemen. After Ghana, the Mali Empire acted in the same way and the Songhay too. These three great empires have dominated together the economic, military, and political history of West Africa for around 900 years.

Let us bear in mind that Ghana had not only succeeded economically and militarily, but also it had a particularly good political administration which was meticulously well organised and structured between the different provinces and the central power.

Political and Social Organization of Ghana Empire

In Kumbi Saleh, the emperor of Ghana reigns over a gigantic territory, we have already precised its surface. This vast empire, whose origin predates the Christian and Muslim eras, which would reach its peak and flourish between the 8th and 12th centuries. Administratively, the Ghana Empire was divided into

---

Wakore is specific for the Soninkes ("Sarakolles"). In the Ivory Coast Forest, The Mandens are called maninka Jula ("Dioula") which means trader. Wangara and Dioula are synonymous meaning the same thing: They design specifically Mandens whose activity is the negoce.

provinces and kingdoms which all depended on the emperor. The latter, with his powerful army, which is estimated much more than 200,000 men, secured, and protected its populations. Governors, kings, ministers, etc. were put in place which permitted him to better lead his people and control his territory. The political organization was clear. After the emperor came 12 patriarch advisers, direct descendants of the emperor's companions. The latter were chosen thanks to their knowledge and their personalities. They first met with the highest authorities to study and discuss all the situations, all the problems and their possible solutions, before the chiefs of wage clans were summoned to undertake the needed action. There were also warlords responsible for organizing the army and overseeing operations on the ground. They were 18 generals called nana. Nine of them rode compulsory red horses and the other 9 rode white horses. After that were the military governors of the provinces, responsible for the regions. There were 12, a figure which corresponded to the number of provinces of the empire. Each province was headed by a governor dealing with or taking charge in local and regional matters. The governors were called *fado*. We also note the existence of senior officers called in the Soninke language the *Hida* as well as scouts. Their mission was to notify the emperor of the presence of the enemy which was in sight: 7 notables were responsible for monitoring the wages so that all prohibitions were respected. Then, they were assisted by 7 assistants. We should also mention the existence of police officials, known as *samasaduaradyuwara*.

Still talking about the social ranking, the people of Ghana consisted of three social categories or classes that are still found in the African countries that were part of this Empire: the nobles or the High-ranking category, the people of caste and the peasants. The reported oral tradition through the case of *Yéréré* whose book we have mentioned (Diterlen and Sylla), enumerated frequently the number of "officials" who oversaw commercial discussions or other negotiations, as assistants to those responsible for religious and family rites. (Weddings, naming ceremonies, circumcisions, funerals, etc.). We are often particularly reminded of the strict prohibitions which resolved the relations that the wages had with the artisans, the other castes, and the captives of the various campaigns against the neighbours afterwards, who are wrongly called slaves. This was not yet the case. We also know the importance of matrimonial unions for which precise rules of kinship must be observed. All residents also had to respect prohibitions associated with the Soninke and Kakolo cults. (Solet, 2004).

Apart from economic, military, political and social organizations, the Ghana Empire had a financial agreement with the use of a common currency: The cowries.

A Common Currency in the Vast Empire of Ghana: Cowries

In West Africa, cowries had been the most popular currency for many centuries. These so-called "money cowries" are shells from a small gastropod that inhabit the tropical waters of the Indian and Pacific oceans. During the time of the Ghanaian Empire and several centuries later, cowries were used as currency. In West Africa, they are even today still being used as jewellery or decorative items, etc. It is thanks to its exchanges with the Muslim world that Ghana has been able to set up a common currency through cowries. Indeed, Arab traders transported cowries from the Maldives islands of the Indian ocean to Egypt, then across the desert to the markets of Africa, the Sahel, and the Savannah. Long after the empire of Ghana, the West Africans continued to use cowries as currency. A long time after Ghana Empire moreover, when Europeans

35

landed on the West African coasts from the 15th century, a period which marked a decisive turning point, a landmark in the history of Africa, the newcomers had noticed that cowries were used as currency between populations. Therefore, when it comes to currency, Europeans tended to prefer cowries to gold. So, in their trade relations with West Africa, the Europeans continued with its use for a long time. For example, in the 16th century, seashells were imported in the ships of Dutch and English traders on the Guinean coast of West Africa. With the advent of the Atlantic slave trade, cowries were among the items exchanged by Europeans. Nowadays, they are still used in West Africa for different things, including decorating clothes, drums, and headdresses, and on ritual carvings such as masks and statuettes. They are also used to foresee the future. You just must visit of Senegal, Mali, Gambia, or the south of Mauritania, to notice it. Indeed, we can see seers throwing a handful of them for their predictions based on how the shells land either with the open side up or down. It is important to point out that cowries were not the only currency used. The exchanges could be made in kind between the populations of the empire. Gold could also be used in certain transactions.

Despite its influence over several centuries, its proven economic prosperity mentioned in various African and foreign sources, its political and cultural unity whose consequences are still visible, its military organization etc., Ghana like all the great civilizations of the world, like all the empires and states that once marked the history of mankind, would experience its decline due to several factors that will be analyzed in this last part.

Ghana's Decline

The Ghana's decline is in the most part due to the same reasons which have made Ghana's prosperity and its influence, its expansion, and its opening to the world as well as the relations established with the Arab Muslim world which also had other hidden ambitions, others than the simple Islamization of Africa. The Muslim advancement in sub-Saharan Africa was indeed going to change the balance of power concerning the relations between Arab Muslims and the populations of the Ghana Empire quite quickly. The peaceful trade exchanges were soon replaced by endless conflicts. On the one hand the Almoravids, these jihadists of medieval times and on the other an army of the emperor of Ghana in loss of unity and motivation, overwhelmed by the fervour and determination of the newcomers or their representatives and allies in North Africa.

Indeed, during the 8th century, the Zanatas and other Berbers in the Moroccan Atlas region became Muslims, and later the Sanhajas were also converted to Islam. The religious conversion had given them all broader trade connections. It then increased the scale and complexity of their trade and generally improved their prosperity. During the century that followed the Soninke takeover of the town of Awdaghost, the Sanhajas became involved in a new dynamic, namely the Almoravid movement. This had a great influence on the propagation of Islam, itself a major factor in the history of West Africa but also as far as Spain and the south of France (the great caliphate al Andalusian). At the beginning of 10th century, the Sanhajas were rulers of Western Sahara, but they were spread over a large area and divided into sub-groups or clans. They lived in various sectors and dominated the trade routes and the salt mines, which also allowed them to benefit from great profits. The subgroups who were living in the southern part of the desert were the Juddalas (or Diouddalas) and the Lamtunas, who bordered the kingdom of Ghana. Awdaghost opposed the Lamtunas and the Soninke. Islam was spreading in the region, but it was weaker and less orthodox in the South than in the

North. The Arab-Muslims did not hesitate to use religion as a pretext to annex all of Ghana if possible. This is the beginning of the end for this centuries-old Empire.

We pointed it out that the main concern of the Almoravids was the strict respect of the discipline of Islam. They wanted that all the rules of this religion to be followed: prayer and fasting, abstention from alcohol (the local fermented drinks made of millet or other grains) and prohibited food, making the pilgrimage to Mecca, and learning the Koran. They were ready to promote these things by force through jihad or armed conflict. This meant that the Almoravids had to have a solid base from which to launch their military campaigns, and that the clans involved had to be unified. They began a campaign to integrate the Masoufas and other Sanhaja people of the southern Sahara into their movement. Some Sanhaja clans continued to rebel, but most of them joined the alliance and were consolidated into an effective political federation of the desert subgroups.

In 1048 the Almoravids became the strongest force or military power in Western Sahara but had still many battles ahead of them. In 1054 they conquered Awdaghost which was belonging to the Soninkés of Ghana. That same year, they reached the North across the Sahara and captured the largest trading town of Sijilmasa, a prosperous town full of history located in Southern Morocco. In 1056, the Almoravids were informed that Sijilmasa was conquered by the Zanatas, its former leaders. Yasin, founder of the movement, and most of his army walked to the North to conquer this city again, but in the south, the Juddala rebelled again. Chief Lamtuna Yahya must have stayed behind to face Juddala and was killed during the battles. His brother Abu Bakr ibn Umar replaced him as a supreme military commander of the Almoravids. Yasin was

38

killed during one of the many Almoravid campaigns in 1059. Once they took control of the Sahara and the northern part of the trade routes, the Almoravid Berbers began their expeditions against the brilliant West African Empire of Ghana in the second half of the 11th century. Less than twenty years later, in 1076, the Berber fighters succeeded in seizing the capital of Ghana Koumbi Saleh, the city that Abu Bakr ben Omar was found of, Ghana. But they were neither numerous nor strong enough to keep and maintain the different kingdoms which formed the Empire gathered. This victory permitted though the Almoravids to occupy a very strategic position, particularly the control of trade ways, which is a blow to the economy of Ghana, whose trans-Saharan trade played a leading role through the various exchanges.

The Emperor of Ghana called on his people to a general mobilisation and support them by demanding the fighters not to give up. This call helped to recapture the city of Koumbi Saleh a few years later in 1087. But the eleven years of occupation, the breakdown and the economic and political disorganisation have resulted in leaving the Empire in a pitiful and very vulnerable situation.

At the end of the 11th century, Ghana was still defeated and remained very weak. The Empire begins to be disorganised, some provinces and kingdoms which are no longer in this federation and get out of it. Thus, it is now the beginning of a slow decline and an unavoidable dislocation. The people of the north of the empire converted by the Almoravids accept the Muslim power and the hegemony of the newcomers, while the populations of the south, for their par who prefer keeping the ancestral African religions, begin a new migration even in the south, especially in forests where Almoravid fighters cannot reach because their horses could be killed by the bites of the Tsetse fly. These are the current people of the southern regions of Ivory Coast, Senegal, the Republic of Ghana and even Benin. Others moved to the East and attempt to reconstruct their lives. These massive departures empty the Empire and result negatively in the life of the Federal State. The army no longer believes and becomes less and less powerful and unable to attract new recruits.

It is in this context that we notice the emergence of small kingdoms or small political entities around the clans in the southern and eastern parts of the empire of Ghana namely the kingdoms of Mali, Diarra, Sosso, etc. In addition, certain black states already Islamized, such as Tekrur (on both banks of the middle valley of the Senegal River), rallied to the Almoravids and suddenly became opponents of Ghana's opponents. Wardjabi, its king, already converted to Islam, and had taken an active part in the holy war trigged by the Almoravids; his son, Labi or Laba, continued this policy of alliance with the Almoravids and fought with them against the Godalas in 1056. (Niane, 1980, 145).

Like Tekrur, the various vassal states of Ghana sometimes waged war against it with the aim of taking back trade routes, controlling the economy (trade, breeding, agriculture, mines, etc.). As a result, one of these vassal kingdoms the Sosso, of the famous king Soumahoro Kanté (Kanteh), for instance succeeded in conquering the capital Koumbi Saleh and putting to an end to the long reign of Wagadu at the beginning of the 13th century. The empire of Ghana which began its terrible decline from the 11the century, was successively dominated by Almoravid, then the Sosso, and finally by the Empire of Mali.

Yet the Ghana Empire remains in the collective memory of African people, as being the first Black State of the medieval epoch. The written sources, the oral tradition, the archaeological research testify it, but also songs are still dedicated to this former Empire[23].

---

[23]The Senegalese group Toure Kunda has well sung the Wagadu through his famous song Soninko: https://www.youtube.com/watch?v=F3a6b8B-g6U

Conclusion

Ghana was the first medieval West African empire founded by Black Africans (the Soninke) who still live in the same geographical area. All sources (Arabs, oral tradition or archaeological) are unanimous on the fact that Ghana was extraordinarily rich in gold, hence its name the "land of gold" by the Arabs. We also know that the trans-Saharan trade had been active and flourishing for several centuries between Ghana and the Maghreb countries before the Almoravids took over Ghana. The latter testifies the stinging denial to those who think that there was no viable or respectful political organization in Africa before the arrival of the Arab conquerors or the European imperialists.

The Ghana empire must be studied again, its history which was over more than ten centuries (both royal and imperial) deserves really to be known by the contemporary African populations and above all to be taught to the young African Generations, so that they could be aware of their unity that is stronger and older than what separates them.

Bibliography

Bathily, Y., *Rois et peuples de l'empire du Ghana : VI-XII siècles*, Bamako, CARPE DIEM, 2018.

Courrier de l'UNESCO, Juin, 1974.

Delafosse, M., *Haut-Sénégal-Niger (Soudan français)*, tome II, l'Histoire, Paris, 1912.

Diagana, M, *La légende du Wagadu, vue par Sia Yatabaré*, Éd. Lansman, the University of Virginia, 1994.

Herskovits, M. J., "Cattle Complex in East Africa", *Dictionary of the Social Sciences*, Oxford, 1926.

Histoire Générale de l'Afrique, vol 3, chapitre 14. 365 "Les Almoravides", chapitre 15 "Commerce et routes en Afrique occidentales" p. 397, 1990.

Gomgnimbou, M., Gayibor, N. L. et Juhé-Beaulaton, D., L'écriture de l'histoire en Afrique : l'oralité toujours en question, Paris Karthala, 2006.

N'Diaye, T. *Mémoire d'errance*, chap. « Empire du Ghana », Ed A3, Paris, 1998.

Solet, B., *Les chemins de Yelimané*, Paris, Éd Hachette 1995.

Sylla, D. et Dieterlen, G., *L'Empire de Ghana*, Paris, Karthala 1992.

https://www.universalis.fr/encyclopedie/empire-du-ghana/4-les-almoravides-et-la-chute-du-ghana/
Bathily, Y, *Kings and People of the Ghana Empire: VI-XII centuries*, Bamako, CARPE, DIEM, 2018
Unesco Magazine, June 1974.

Delafosse, M., *High-Senegal- Niger (French Sudan) History Tome II*, Paris, 1912.

Diagana, M., *The Legend of Wagadu seen by/described by Sia Yatabare*, Ed. Lansman, the University of Virginia, 1994.

Herskovits, M. J., "Cattle complex in East Africa" *Dictionary of the social sciences*, Oxford, 1926.

General History of Africa, vol.3, chapter 14. 365 "The Almoravids" chapter 15 "trade and roads in west Africa.

Gomgnimbou, M., Gayibor, N.L and Juhe-Beaulaton, D, *Writing the History of Africa: The topical question of Orality*, Paris, Karthala, 2006

N'Diaye, T. *Wandering Memory, chapter* "Ghana Empire" Ed. A3, Paris.1998

Solet, B., The Yelimane Roads, Paris, Ed. Hachette 1995.

Sylla, D. and Dieterlen G., *The Ghana Empire*, Paris, Karthala 1992.

Book Summary

Ghana Empire is one of the earliest known political formations in West Africa. Nicknamed the "land of gold", Ghana had acquired a preeminent role in the Sahel and Savannah space in West Africa. This book traces the glorious history of this brilliant medieval empire, in particular its origins, its expansion from kingdom (Wagadu) to a vast empire (Ghana), its prosperous economy, political unity, social cohesion, cultural area and especially the economic and trade relations with the Muslims East and Mediterranean Europe.

Author

Historian, researcher and writer, Amadou BA holds a Doctorate in history (specialization in colonial history of Africa), a master's in political science (specialization in African politics) and a certificate in teaching. Currently, he teaches African history at Nipissing University (North Bay Ontario in Canada). He also teaches in the Faculty of Education and in the Department of Political Science at Laurentian University (Sudbury, Ontario). Amadou BA has written other books on his own: The forgotten history of the contribution of Black slaves and Soldiers to the Building of Canada (1604-1945) published in 2019, West Africa soldiers in the conquest and colonization of the Great Island 1895- 1960, published in 2012. Amadou BA is also a speaker, notably sharing his research on Black history in Canada and North America.

www.ingramcontent.com/pod-product-compliance
Lightning Source LLC
Chambersburg PA
CBHW071938020426
42331CB00010B/2922